The Boublil–Schönberg Collection
Show Hits

Twelve great show songs ideal for auditions

Music Sales Group

London/New York/Paris/Sydney/Copenhagen/Berlin/Madrid/Tokyo

Published by
Wise Publications
8/9 Frith Street, London W1D 3JB, UK.

Exclusive Distributors:
Music Sales Limited
Distribution Centre, Newmarket Road, Bury St Edmunds, Suffolk IP33 3YB, UK.
Music Sales Corporation
257 Park Avenue South, New York, NY10010, USA.
Music Sales Pty Limited
120 Rothschild Avenue, Rosebery, NSW 2018, Australia.

Order No. AM983719
ISBN 1-84609-230-2

Cover design by Chloë Alexander
Printed in the United Kingdom

Your Guarantee of Quality
As publishers, we strive to produce every book to the highest commercial
standards.
This book has been carefully designed to minimise awkward page turns
and to make playing from it a real pleasure.
Particular care has been given to specifying acid-free, neutral-sized paper made
from pulps which have not been elemental chlorine bleached. This pulp is from
farmed sustainable forests and was produced with special regard for the
environment.
Throughout, the printing and binding have been planned to ensure a sturdy,
attractive publication which should give years of enjoyment.
If your copy fails to meet our high standards, please inform us and we will
gladly replace it.

www.musicsales.com

Also available:
The Boublil–Schönberg Collection
Show Hits
Audition Songs Male Edition
Twelve more show songs specially arranged for male singers complete with
backing tracks on CD.

Includes...
The American Dream Miss Saigon
Bring Him Home Les Misérables
Bui-Doi Miss Saigon
Do You Hear The People Sing? Les Misérables
Empty Chairs At Empty Tables Les Misérables
Here Comes The Morning Martin Guerre
I Will Make You Proud Martin Guerre
Martin Guerre Martin Guerre
Master Of The House Les Misérables
Stars Les Misérables
Who Am I? Les Misérables
Why God Why? Miss Saigon

Order No. AM983708

Castle On A Cloud

Music and lyrics by
Claude-Michel Schönberg, Alain Boublil,
Jean-Marc Natel & Herbert Kretzmer

3. There is a la - dy all in white ___ holds me and sings a lul - la - by. She's

nice to see and she's soft to touch; she says 'Cos - ette, I love you very much.' I know a place where no-one's

lost, I know a place where no - one cries.

Cry - ing at all is not al - lowed, Not in my cast - le on a cloud.

poco rit.

5

How Many Tears?

Music and lyrics by
Claude-Michel Schönberg, Alain Boublil
& Stephen Clark

I Dreamed A Dream

Music and lyrics by
Claude-Michel Schönberg, Alain Boublil,
Jean-Marc Natel & Herbert Kretzmer

I dreamed that God would be for - giv - ing.
No song un - sung, no wine un - tast - ed.

But the ti-gers come at night, With their voi-ces soft as thun - der;

As they tear your hope a - part, As they turn your dream to shame.

3. He slept a sum - mer by my side,

He filled my days with end-less won-der.___ He took my child-hood in his

stride, But he was gone when au-tumn came.

4. And still I dreamed he'd come to me, That we would live the years to-

-geth - er.___ But there are dreams that can-not be,

I'd Give My Life For You

Music and lyrics by
Claude-Michel Schönberg, Alain Boublil
& Richard Maltby Jr.

but there's just moon-light on my bed.

Was he a ghost, was he a lie

that made my bo-dy laugh and cry?

Then by my side the proof I see,

his lit-tle one. Gods of the sun

bring him to me.

You will be who you want to be.

You

molto rall.   *a tempo*

sub. ***p***

maestoso

I Saw Him Once

Music and lyrics by
Claude-Michel Schönberg, Alain Boublil,
Jean-Marc Natel & Herbert Kretzmer

Now That I've Seen Her

Music and lyrics by
Claude-Michel Schönberg, Alain Boublil
& Richard Maltby Jr.

Moderato

The Movie In My Mind

Music and lyrics by
Claude-Michel Schönberg, Alain Boublil
& Richard Maltby Jr.

Leila Lerari

KING LEAR..

ACT 1, SCENE 1, PAGE 3

Goneril:
Regan:
Cordelia: leila
King Lear: douvelle

Goneril: Sir I love you more than words can say. I love you more than eyesight, space and freedom, beyond wealth or anything of value. I love you as much as life itself and as much as status, health, beauty or honour. I love you as much as any child has ever loved her father, with a love too deep to be spoken of. I love you more than any answer to the question "How much?"

Cordelia: (to herself) What will I say? I can only love and be silent.

Lear: I give you all this land, from this line to that one - dense forests, fertile fields rivers rich with fish, wide meadows. This land will belong to your and Albany's children forever. - And now what does my second daughter, Regan, the wife of cornwall have to say? Tell me.

Regan: Sir, I'm made of the same stuff as my sister and consider myself just as good as she is. She's described my feelings of love for you precisely, but her description falls a little short of the truth. I reject completely any joy except my love for you, and I find that only your majesty's love makes me happy.

Cordelia: (to herself) Poor me, what am I going to say now? But I'm not poor in love — my love is bigger than my words are.

Lear: You are your heirs hereby receive this large third of our lovely kingdom, no smaller in area or value than what I gave Goneril —Now, you, my youngest daughter, my joy, courted by the rich rulers of France and Burgundy, what can you tell me that will make me give you a bigger part of my kingdom than I gave your sisters? Speak.

Cordelia: Nothing my Lord.

Lear: Nothing?

Cordelia: Nothing.

http://nfs.sparknotes.com/lear/page_8.html

Goneril:
Regan:
Cordelia: Leila
King Lear: douvelle

TRANSLATION!
:KING:
:LEAR: ACT 1, SCENE 1, PAGE 4

Leila lerari

Lear: Come on, "nothing" will get you nothing. Try again

Cordelia: I'm unlucky. I don't have a talent for putting my hearts feelings into words. I love you as a child should love her father, neither more nor less.

Lear: What are you saying, Cordelia? Revise your statement, or you may damage your inheritance.

Cordelia: My lord, you brought me up and loved me, and I'm giving back just as I should: I obey you, love you and honour you. How can my sisters speak the truth when they say they love only you? Don't they love their husbands too? Hopefully when I get married, I'll give my husband half my love and half my sense of duty. I'm sure I'll never get married in the way my sisters say they're married, loving their father only.

Lear: But do you mean what you're saying??

Cordelia: Yes my lord.

Lear: So young + so cruel?

Cordelia: So young, my lord, and honest.

Lear: Then thats the way it'll be. The truth will be all the inheritance you get. I swear by the sacred sun, by the mysterious moon, and by all the planets that rule our lives, that I disown you know as my daughter. As of now there are no family ties between us, and I consider you a stranger to me. foreign savages who eat their own children for dinner will be as close to my heart as you ex-daughter of mine.

30

rit.

rall.

On My Own

Music and lyrics by
Claude-Michel Schönberg, Alain Boublil,
Jean-Marc Natel, Herbert Kretzmer,
John Caird & Trevor Nunn

And now I'm all a-lone a-gain; no-where to go, no one to turn to.

The Sacred Bird

Music and lyrics by
Claude-Michel Schönberg, Alain Boublil
& Richard Maltby Jr.

I will nev - er be far   but, my son, it's your turn

to   know   your   fath - er's   love.

I know now why I   came to this earth,   it's   so you find your place.

But   for   that   I   must   leave_____   your   em - brace.

Someone

Music and lyrics by
Claude-Michel Schönberg, Alain Boublil
& Stephen Clark

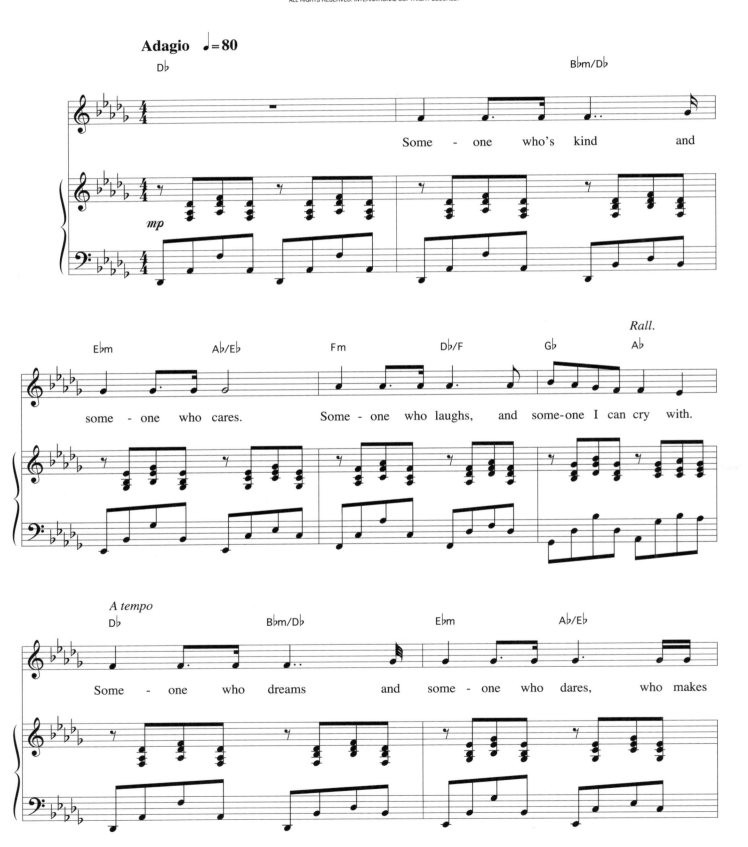

When Will Someone Hear?

Music and lyrics by
Claude-Michel Schönberg, Alain Boublil
& Stephen Clark

When will some-one hear? Love that once was close,— faith that once was clear.—

Now all I've known and all I've loved is all I have to grieve.—

All that I've be-gun, all that I be-lieve is just a-no-ther bro-ken dream.—

When will some-one hear? They seem so strong,

Quatre Saisons Pour Un Amour

Music and lyrics by
Claude-Michel Schönberg, Alain Boublil,
Raymond Jeannot & Jean-Max Rivière

1. Les cris d'un vol d'oi-seaux à ma fe-
2. Au fils du temps qui nous sé-pare sans

-nê - tre.
ces - se.

Ap-pel-lent en vain le so-leil à pa-tris-
Mon coeur ap-prend la peur et la

-raî - tre.
-tes - se.

Les doigts sa-tin du vent dans les nu-
Sous quel so-leil de-main se-rons-nous

53

123456789

Make a big impression with these song collections for auditions...

Audition Songs for Female Singers

Don't Cry For Me Argentina...
plus Adelaide's Lament, Big Spender; Heaven Help My Heart; I Cain't Say No; I Will Survive; Out Here On My Own; Saving All My Love For You; Someone To Watch Over Me; The Wind Beneath My Wings. ORDER NO. AM92587

I Dreamed A Dream...
plus Another Suitcase In Another Hall; Fame; If I Were A Bell; Miss Byrd; Save The Best For Last; Someone Else's Story; There Are Worse Things I Could Do; What I Did For Love; You Can Always Count On Me. ORDER NO. AM950224

Memory...
plus Can't Help Lovin' Dat Man; Crazy; Diamonds Are A Girl's Best Friend; Now That I've Seen Her; Show Me Heaven; That Ole Devil Called Love; The Winner Takes It All; Wishing You Were Somehow Here Again; The Reason. ORDER NO. AM955284

I Don't Know How To Love Him...
plus As Long As He Needs Me; Constant Craving; Feeling Good; I Say A Little Prayer; If My Friends Could See Me Now; It's Oh So Quiet; Killing Me Softly With His Song; Tell Me It's Not True; You Must Love Me. ORDER NO. AM955295

Beautiful...
plus Complicated; Don't Know Why; For What It's Worth; I'm Gonna Getcha Good!; Kiss Kiss; No More Drama; One Day I'll Fly Away; A Thousand Miles; Whenever, Wherever. ORDER NO. AM977130

Murder On The Dancefloor...
plus Castles In The Sky; Heaven; Hungry; I Turn To You; Set You Free; Silence; Touch Me; Who Do You Love Now? ORDER NO. AM959156

Chart Hits
Against All Odds (Take A Look At Me Now); American Pie; ...Baby One More Time; Breathless; It Feels So Good; Man! I Feel Like A Woman; My Love Is Your Love; Pure Shores; Rise; Sing It Back. ORDER NO. AM963765

90's Hits
History Repeating; I Will Always Love You; Never Ever; Perfect Moment; Search For The Hero; That Don't Impress Me Much; Torn; 2 Become 1; What Can I Do; You Gotta Be. ORDER NO. AM963776

Hits of the 90s
All Mine; Baby One More Time; Black Velvet; Chains; Don't Speak; From A Distance; Hero; Lovefool; Road Rage; What Can I Do. ORDER NO. AM966658

Blues
Cry Me A River; Black Coffee; Fine And Mellow (My Man Don't Love Me); The Lady Sings The Blues; Lover Man (Oh Where Can You Be); God Bless' The Child; Moonglow; Natural Blues; Please Send Me Someone To Love; Solitude. ORDER NO. AM966669

Classic Soul
Don't Make Me Over; I Just Want To Make Love To You; Midnight Train To Georgia; Nutbush City Limits; Private Number; Rescue me; Respect; Son Of A Preacher Man; Stay With Me Baby; (Take A Little) Piece Of My Heart. ORDER NO. AM966670

R&B Hits
Ain't It Funny; AM To PM; Family Affair; Freak Like Me; Get The Party Started; How Come You Don't Call Me; Shoulda Woulda Coulda; Sweet Baby; Survivor; What About Us? ORDER NO. AM967351

Cabaret Songs
Big Spender; Cabaret; Falling In Love Again; I Am A Vamp; If My Friends Could See Me Now; The Ladies Who Lunch; Maybe This Time; Mein Herr; No Regrets (Non, Je Ne Regrette Rien); Take Me To Your Heart Again (La Vie En Rose). ORDER NO. AM958881

More Audition Songs for Kids
The Bare Necessities; Can You Feel The Love Tonight; Food, Glorious Food; Happy Talk; I Have A Dream; Maybe; Reach; Starlight Express; What If; You've Got A Friend In Me. ORDER NO. AM966636

ALL TITLES AVAILABLE FROM GOOD MUSIC RETAILERS OR, IN CASE OF DIFFICULTY, CONTACT THE MARKETING DEPTARTMENT, MUSIC SALES LIMITED, NEWMARKET ROAD, BURY ST. EDMUNDS, SUFFOLK IP33 3YB marketing@musicsales.co.uk

CD Backing Tracks

1. Castle On A Cloud
(Schönberg/Boublil/Natel/Kretzmer)
SACEM/Alain Boublil Overseas Limited.

2. How Many Tears?
(Schönberg/Boublil/Clark/Hardy)
Alain Boublil Overseas Limited.

3. I Dreamed A Dream
(Schönberg/Boublil/Natel/Kretzmer)
SACEM/Alain Boublil Overseas Limited.

4. I'd Give My Life For You
(Schönberg/Boublil/Maltby)
Alain Boublil Overseas Limited.

5. I Saw Him Once
(Schönberg/Boublil/Natel/Kretzmer)
SACEM/Alain Boublil Overseas Limited.

6. Now That I've Seen Her
(Schönberg/Boublil/Maltby)
Alain Boublil Overseas Limited.

7. The Movie In My Mind
(Schönberg/Boublil/Maltby)
Alain Boublil Overseas Limited.

8. On My Own
(Schönberg/Boublil/Natel/Kretzmer/Caird/Nunn)
SACEM/Alain Boublil Overseas Limited.

9. The Sacred Bird
(Schönberg/Boublil/Maltby)
Alain Boublil Overseas Limited.

10. Someone
(Schönberg/Boublil/Clark/Hardy)
Alain Boublil Overseas Limited.

11. When Will Someone Hear?
(Schönberg/Boublil/Clark)
Alain Boublil Overseas Limited.

12. Quatre Saisons Pour Un Amour
(Schönberg/Boublil/Rivière/Jeannot)
SACEM/Alain Boublil Overseas Limited.

To remove your CD from the plastic sleeve,
lift the small lip to break the perforations.
Replace the disc after use for convenient storage.